sibling relationships in the animal world

sisters & brothers

steve jenkins & robin page

houghton mifflin company • boston 2008

Playing together, working together, arguing, fighting — sometimes animal brothers and sisters act a lot like human siblings. Other creatures have more unusual relationships. They may be identical quadruplets, or have only sisters. Some have hundreds, thousands, or even millions of brothers and sisters. There are animal brothers that fight to the death, and others that are companions for life. In this book you can read about some of the ways animal siblings get along — or not. At the back of the book you can find out more about each creature's size, what it eats, and where it lives.

Bringing up baby.

Like humans, **African elephants** are usually born singly. Elephants weigh 200 pounds (440 kilograms) or more at birth, but even a youngster this size isn't safe from lions and other predators. If a baby elephant wanders away from its herd, an older sister will often act as a babysitter and guide it back to safety. A typical elephant herd includes twelve to fifteen family members led by an older female. Young elephants are well cared for until they are about twelve years old. At this age, males leave the group to live on their own. Females, however, stay with the herd and help take care of their younger siblings, bathing them, feeding them, and keeping them safe.

Let's
hold
on!

Two tiny bats hold on to their mother's fur, one under each of her wings. They hang on while she hunts and stay safely in place as she folds down her long ears to sleep. **Gould's long-eared bats** are almost always born as twins. They stay together, clinging to their mother, until they are about four months old. When these small mammals begin to fly on their own, they will hunt and navigate using echolocation — making a rapid series of high-pitched calls and listening for the echoes. In this way, bats can catch insects and avoid obstacles even when flying in complete darkness.

Twins

Exactly alike.

Nine-banded armadillos are always born as identical quadruplets — four brothers or four sisters. They are clones, perfect copies of one another, so they are exactly alike down to their toenails. Armadillos are born with their eyes open and can walk when they are just a few hours old. The quads stay with their mother for several months before setting off on their own. When full grown, this armored mammal is about the size of a small dog. If it is threatened, an armadillo can run, jump, or swim surprisingly quickly. If all else fails, it rolls itself up into an armored ball.

Girls rule!

New Mexico whiptail lizards have only sisters. There are no brothers, because there are no male whiptails. All the sisters in a whiptail community are identical. They are also identical to their mother, their grandmother, and all their female ancestors. Female whiptails don't need to find a mate to produce offspring. Plants often reproduce this way, but animals rarely do. Reproduction without a male does have some advantages, since whiptails don't have to spend any time or energy finding a mate. However, since all the lizards in one of these family groups are exactly the same, a disease or change in habitat that is fatal to one animal could wipe out the entire community.

Sisters

Two **naked mole rats,** hairless and nearly blind, meet in an underground tunnel. They stop and sniff each other. Then one mole rat lies flat on the tunnel floor while the other walks right over its back. These two rodents are siblings. There may be hundreds of animals in this colony, and almost all of them are brothers and sisters. They are the offspring of a single female, the queen. She is the only member of the colony that can have babies. Animal societies of this sort are common in the insect world but are very unusual among mammals. Mole rats use their large front teeth to dig a complex tunnel system, their colony's home. Within each colony there is a strict system of social status, or rank, based on a member's age and occupation. When two mole rats meet, the lower status brother or sister has to lie flat on the floor to let its sibling pass by.

Hundreds of siblings.

Mommy's busy right now . . .

Millions of **termite** brothers and sisters may
live together in a single mound, or nest.
These mounds, the largest non-man-made
structures in the world, are sometimes as tall
as a four-story building. A single female termite, the queen,
may produce as many as 30,000 eggs a day for her colony.
Every termite sibling has a job to do. Workers repair the nest,
collect food, and take care of the queen, who is so heavy that
she can't move on her own. Soldiers are larger and use their
huge jaws to defend the nest against attack. Termites look a
bit like ants but are closely related to cockroaches.

A very large family

Young **grizzly bear** brothers like to fight. At first, they are only playing. As they get older, however, their tussles become more serious. Grizzly bears are born in litters of two or three cubs. They stay close to their mother for about a year. When the mother leaves, the young bears may stay together for another year, searching for food and sleeping through the winter in a furry pile. As a male cub gets older, he wants to establish and defend his own territory. Grizzly bear brothers fight increasingly fierce battles until the losing male cub leaves to search for territory somewhere else. The brothers usually separate before one of them gets seriously hurt.

Spotted hyenas are distantly related to dogs, and their babies look like playful puppies as they nip and growl. Don't be fooled, though — full-grown hyenas are among the fiercest animals on earth, and this sibling fighting is serious. Spotted hyenas live and hunt in packs. Hyena pups are usually born two at a time. If they are brother and sister, they will probably get along and survive to grow up and join the pack. However, if a litter includes two brothers or two sisters, the pups begin to fight at an early age. Often the weaker sibling is so badly injured in these battles that it will die. This seems cruel, but it helps guarantee that only the most aggressive hyenas survive and grow up, keeping the pack tough and strong.

Family
life
is
tough.

Young **black widow spiders,** called spiderlings, emerge from a silken egg sac about the size of a grape. These spiderlings start out with as many as 700 brothers and sisters, but only a few survive. Black widows are cannibals. As soon as they hatch, the strongest spiders begin to eat their weaker brothers and sisters. Adult males and spiderlings are not dangerous to people, but the female black widow is the most venomous spider in North America. Her bite is painful to humans, and can be fatal. The black widow gets its name from the female's occasional habit of devouring the male after mating with him.

I'm having my family for dinner . . .

Sibling rivalry

Two young **cheetahs** stalk each other, then leap into the air, snarling and swatting. They are sisters, part of a litter of five cubs. They are playing, but their games have a purpose. An adult cheetah runs faster than any other land animal. It can run at speeds of 70 miles (113 kilometers) per hour, but only for a short distance. Cheetahs hunt antelopes — animals that are also very fast and able to run much farther than a big cat. If a cheetah doesn't bring down its prey quickly, it won't catch anything. Hunting games help these young cats get ready to catch their own food. The mother cheetah leaves her cubs to fend for themselves when they are about eighteen months old. The siblings stay together for another six months. At that point the sisters leave to start their own families, but the brothers hunt together throughout their lives.

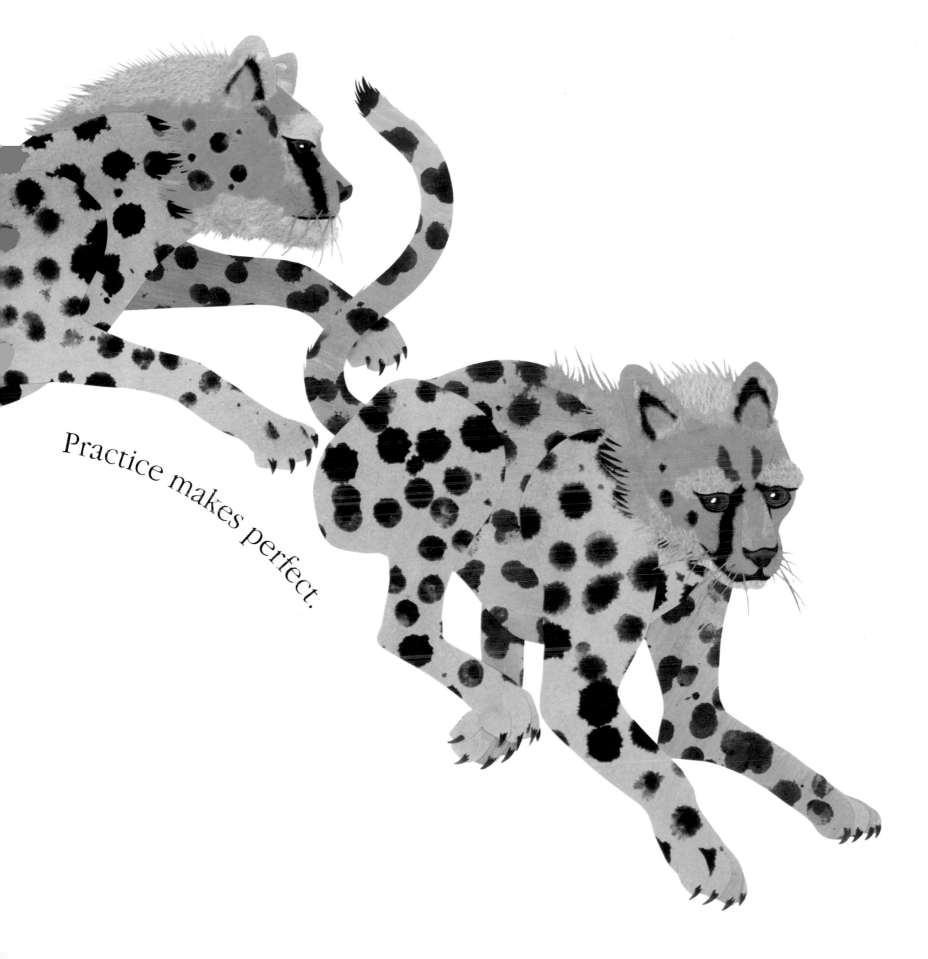

Practice makes perfect.

Isn't
it your
turn to
be the
pigeon?

As it soars high above the ground, a young
peregrine falcon is attacked by another bird.
A diving hawk or eagle would be bad news, but
it's just the falcon's sister, practicing her hunting
technique. Peregrine falcons are the fastest living things
on earth. They reach speeds of 200 miles per hour (320
kilometers per hour) in a hunting dive, or stoop. When a
falcon strikes a duck or pigeon at these speeds, the smaller
bird is instantly stunned or killed. Hitting a moving target
in a high-speed dive is not an easy thing to do, and young
peregrine falcons need lots of practice before they can hunt
for themselves. With their brothers and sisters, they take
turns pretending to be hunter and prey. Luckily, they are
careful to not really injure each other.

Learning together

Wild turkey brothers are lifelong companions. One male bird, usually the largest, is the leader. His brothers help him attract a female turkey by strutting and displaying their tail feathers. They also help him chase away rival males. Wild turkeys are not the same birds as the domestic turkeys found in supermarkets. They are smaller, smarter, and faster than their farm-raised cousins. A wild turkey mother lays ten to twelve eggs in the spring. After they hatch, the young birds stay with their mother and siblings for a year. The females leave to begin their own families, and the males begin their life as a band of brothers.

Friends for life.

Busy,
busy,
busy.

Four young **beavers** — two brothers and two sisters — take turns cutting down a tree, gnawing through the trunk with chisel-like front teeth. Next, they chew off the branches and drag them into a nearby pond. There the young beavers swim to the bottom and, working together, weigh the branches down with stones. When the pond freezes over in the winter, the tree's tender bark will feed the beaver family. There are three to five baby beavers, or kits, in a litter. Beaver siblings stay with their parents for two years, helping to build dams, repair their lodge, and collect food.

Baby **Nile crocodiles** begin to cooperate even before they hatch. A mother crocodile buries forty or fifty eggs in a large pile of mud and leaves. A baby can't get out of this nest on its own, so it calls for its mother from inside its egg. The voice of one small crocodile would not be heard, but all the babies cry out together in a cheeping chorus. The mother hears their cries, uncovers the eggs, and rolls them gently in her mouth to help the babies get out of their shells. Crocodiles also work together after they hatch, using a special cry to warn their brothers and sisters of danger. When they hear this cry, the babies all chime in, rush to a nearby parent, and climb into its open mouth. There they hide until it is safe to come out.

Danger!
Let's hide!

For the first few weeks of their lives, **great crested grebe** (*greeb*) chicks ride on their mother's back as she swims, hiding beneath her feathers. Soon the young birds get too large for her to carry, and she shakes them off. Now the chicks must swim on their own. As they paddle around, the young birds instinctively stay close to their brothers and sisters, and they all cluster around their mother. The chicks will leave the family group when they are about ten weeks old.

Sink or swim.

One big happy family.

After a mother **cichlid** (*sick*-lid) lays her eggs, she picks them up and carries them in her mouth to keep them safe. Sometimes, she gets more than she bargained for. A cuckoo catfish, lurking nearby, may have left some of her own eggs in the cichlid's nest. If the mother cuckoo catfish gets a chance, she will dart in and eat some of the cichlid's eggs the moment they are laid. Then she puts her own eggs in their place. The mother cichlid picks up the catfish eggs along with her own. She protects all of the eggs, and when they hatch, she raises the baby catfish alongside her own children. The young cichlids and their adopted catfish siblings swim into the mother cichlid's mouth whenever danger threatens.

When the eggs in a myna bird's nest hatch, myna parents sometimes find that one of the chicks is much larger than the other baby birds. It is an **Asian koel** (*koh*-uhl), a bird that lays a single egg in the nests of other birds. The myna parents take care of the egg and feed the koel chick after it hatches. The baby koel is twice the size of the mynas' own chicks, and its foster parents may become exhausted finding enough food for it. Sometimes the myna chicks are pushed out of their nest by their adopted sibling. Often, however, the two different kinds of birds are raised together. When the koel is old enough to fly, it leaves the myna family behind.

Moving
in.

Giant anteaters are born singly and stay with their mother for about two years. A baby anteater can walk when it is four weeks old, but it spends much of its first year riding on its mother's back. A young anteater goes off to live on its own before its mother has another baby, so it will never know a brother or sister. This shaggy mammal will be about the size of a large dog when it's full grown. A giant anteater will feed on ants, but it prefers termites. With its long, sticky tongue it can slurp up 30,000 insects a day.

I'm tired – carry me!

African elephants are the largest living land animals. An adult male stands about 10 feet (3 meters) tall at the shoulder and weighs about 12,000 pounds (5,443 kilograms). An elephant may eat 600 pounds (272 kilograms) of roots, leaves, and fruit a day. African elephants live in grasslands and forests in central and southern Africa.

Gould's long-eared bats are found in eastern Australia, where they frequently roost in hollow trees. Only about 2½ inches (6 ½ centimeters) long, these small bats fly near the ground, scooping insects from the air and eating them as they fly.

The **nine-banded armadillo** is found from Argentina to the southern United States. It grows to 30 inches (76 centimeters) in length and weighs about 14 pounds (6½ kilograms). Armadillos dig burrows, often near ponds and streams. They feed on worms, grubs, and insects.

The **New Mexico whiptail lizard** grows to be 9 inches (23 centimeters) long. Unlike many desert animals, these fast-moving, insect-eating lizards are active in the daytime. Whiptails live in the shelter of rocks and bushes in the southwestern United States and northern Mexico.

Naked mole rats, also known as sand puppies, live in the grasslands of eastern Africa. They are about 3½ inches (9 centimeters) long. They feed on large tubers, or roots, that they discover while digging tunnels. Unlike other mammals, naked mole rats are cold blooded. Strangely, they are also unable to feel pain in their skin.

There are more than 2,500 different kinds of **termites,** found on every continent except Antarctica. They live in underground nests or large aboveground structures made of mud and saliva. Most termites feed on wood pulp. Some eat a special fungus that they grow and tend inside their nests. Typical worker termites are about ¼ inch (6 millimeters) long, but some termite queens may reach 5 inches (12½ centimeters) in length. People

in many parts of the world consider termite queens a tasty delicacy.

Grizzly bears live in the northwestern United States and Canada. Males can weigh as much as 1,500 pounds (680 kilograms), making them one of the largest predators on earth. They are omnivores, eating roots, nuts, insects, fish, and mammals as large as a moose. These bears are powerful, athletic animals. A grizzly can run as fast as a horse, swim, and — despite what many people believe — climb trees. Humans are sometimes attacked and killed by grizzlies.

Spotted hyenas are sometimes called laughing hyenas because their strange high-pitched bark sounds like human laughter. Males are larger than females and may weigh as much as 135 pounds (61 kilograms). Hyenas are accomplished hunters as well as scavengers. They kill antelopes, zebras, and wildebeests, and their jaws are so powerful that they can consume almost every part of their prey, even the bones and hooves.

Hyenas also eat lizards, rodents, insects, and the remains of other predators' kills. They live in central and southern Africa.

Black widow spiders are found in most warm regions of the world. They build their nests on the underside of rocks and plants and inside buildings. The black widow's web is strong, but — unlike the webs of many other spiders — it is constructed with no recognizable pattern. The female black widow is about twice the size of the male. Including her legs, she's about 1½ inches (4 centimeters) across. Black widows eat insects that become ensnared in their webs.

Cheetahs live in isolated areas throughout Africa. They are endangered, and their numbers have fallen sharply in the past few decades. An adult cheetah is about 6½ feet (2 meters) long from nose to tail. Cheetahs hunt small antelopes, rabbits, and birds. Like most cats, they eat only meat. Running flat out, a cheetah can accelerate from 0 to 40 miles per hour (64 kilometers per hour) in three strides.

Peregrine falcons are about 18 inches (46 centimeters) long. They live on every continent except Antarctica, usually along coasts and rivers or in the mountains. These raptors hunt waterfowl and other birds, but will eat small mammals and reptiles. Peregrine falcons also make their homes in big cities, where they nest on tall buildings and feed on pigeons and starlings.

Wild turkeys eat grass, nuts, seeds, and berries. Sometimes they will eat frogs, snakes, and other small animals. Male turkeys weigh an average of 20 pounds (9 kilograms). Females are smaller, about half the weight of males. Wild turkeys can fly as fast as 50 miles per hour (80 kilometers per hour) for short distances. They are found in many of the temperate regions of North America.

Beavers live in North America and Europe. They are animal engineers, constructing dams and lodges with sticks and mud. A beaver lodge has an underwater entrance to keep other animals out. The beaver is the world's second-largest rodent (the South American capybara is the largest). It can be four feet (122 centimeters) long, tail included, and weigh as much as 70 pounds (32 kilograms). Beavers eat tree bark, leaves, roots, and water plants.

A large **Nile crocodile** can grow to be 18 feet (5½ meters) long and weigh more than 1,000 pounds (450 kilograms). These dangerous predators live in rivers and lakes in central and southern Africa and eat fish, turtles, antelopes, zebras — just about any animal, including a human, that gets near the water. The only animals safe from crocodile attack are full-grown elephants and hippopotamuses. Crocodiles can stay underwater for as long as two hours.

The **European shrew** is about 2¾ inches (70 millimeters) long. They may be tiny, but shrews are fierce hunters. They consume nearly their own body weight in food every day, catching and eating insects, worms, frogs, and small reptiles. They live in burrows in meadows and forests throughout Europe.

Great crested grebes can paddle, swim, and dive almost as soon as they hatch. These colorful waterfowl live in lakes throughout Europe and Asia. They eat fish, frogs, crayfish, and insects. Adult grebes are about 20 inches (51 centimeters) long.

There are hundreds of varieties of **cichlids** (*sick*-lids), freshwater fish that live in Africa and South America. Cichlids that carry their eggs and young in their mouths are called mouthbrooders and are most common in African lakes. The cichlid in this book is about 5 inches (13 centimeters) long. It eats water plants and algae.

Cuckoo catfish live in lakes in eastern Africa. They grow to 11 inches (28 centimeters) in length. These fish are parasitic brooders — they rely on cichlids to take care of their eggs and raise their young. Cuckoo catfish eat fish eggs, snails, and insects.

The **Asian koel** (*koh*-uhl), a member of the cuckoo family, lives in the woodlands of southern Asia. It is about 18 inches (46 centimeters) long and feeds on insects and small animals. Like cuckoo catfish, koels are parasitic brooders and use other bird parents to raise their young.

The **common myna** is able to imitate human speech and is sometimes called the talking myna. It lives in India and Southeast Asia. About 4½ inches (11½ centimeters) long, this songbird eats insects and fruit.

Giant anteaters live in the grasslands and forests of Central and South America. With its bushy tail, a giant anteater may be 6½ feet (2 meters) long. Giant anteaters and pangolins, their armored cousins, are the only mammals without teeth. The anteater has a two-foot-long tongue that can be thrust out and pulled back in 150 times a minute. The insects it catches with this sticky tongue are crushed against the inside of its mouth.

For Jeffrey — S.J.

For Doris, Donna, Scott, and Barbara Dell — R.P.

Additional Reading

Caras, Roger. *The Private Lives of Animals.* New York: Grosset & Dunlap, 1974.

Cogger, Dr. Harold G., Joseph Forshaw, and Dr. Edward G. Zweifel, eds.
 The Encyclopedia of Animals. San Francisco: Fog City Press, 1993.

Hare, Dr. Tony. *Animal Fact File.* New York: Checkmark Books, 1999.

Parker, Steve, ed. *Wildlife Factfinder.* Bath, U.K.: Dempsey Parr, 1999.

Penny, Malcolm. *Alligators & Crocodiles.* New York: Crescent Books, 1991.

Rees, Robin, ed. *The Way Nature Works.* New York: MacMillan Publishing Co., 1992.

Richard, Bryan. *The Encyclopedia of North American Mammals.* Bath, U.K.:
 Paragon Publishing, 2004.

The text of this book is set in ITC Adobe Garamond Light.
The illustrations are cut- and torn-paper collage.

Library of Congress Cataloging-in-Publication Data

Jenkins, Steve, 1952–

Sisters and brothers : sibling relationships in the animal world / written by Steve Jenkins and Robin Page ; illustrated by
Steve Jenkins.

 p. cm. Includes bibliographical references and index. ISBN 978-0-618-37596-7 (alk. paper)

1. Animals—Juvenile literature. 2. Brothers and sisters—Juvenile literature. I. Page, Robin, 1957– II. Title.

QL49.J456 2008 591.56'3—dc22

2007034305

Printed in China
SCP 10 9 8 7 6 5 4 3 2 1